DAYS OF
COURAGE
THE LITTLE ROCK STORY

BY RICHARD KELSO

ALEX HALEY,
GENERAL EDITOR

Illustrations by Mel Williges

RSVP
**RAINTREE
STECK-VAUGHN**
P U B L I S H E R S
The Steck-Vaughn Company

Austin, Texas

This book is dedicated to those who began the struggle, and to those who have continued it. Grateful acknowledgement to the staff members of the Schomburg Center for Research in Black Culture, and to the guidance of Rick Larios.

Published by Steck-Vaughn Company.

Text, illustrations, and cover art copyright © 1993 by Dialogue Systems, Inc., 627 Broadway, New York, New York 10012. All rights reserved.

Cover Art by Kye Carbone

Printed in the United States of America

6 7 8 9   LB   01   00   99

Library of Congress Cataloging-in-Publication Data

Kelso, Richard, 1942–
    Days of courage : the Little Rock story / by Richard Kelso: illustrations by Mel Williges.
        p.   cm. — (Stories of America)
    Summary: Describes the experiences of the "Little Rock Nine," the first black students to begin the integration of schools in Arkansas in 1957.
        ISBN 0-8114-7230-2. — ISBN 0-8114-8070-4 (pbk.)
        1. School integration—Arkansas—Little Rock—History—20th century—Juvenile literature. 2. Central High School (Little Rock, Ark.)—History—20th century—Juvenile literature. 3. Afro-American students—Education, Secondary—Arkansas—Little Rock—History—20th century—Juvenile literature. [1. School integration—Arkansas—History. 2. Afro-Americans—Civil rights—Arkansas. 3. Race relations.] I. Williges, Mel, ill. II. Title. III. Series.
    LC214.323.L58K45   1993
    370.19'342—dc20   92-12805
                                                                            CIP
                                                                            AC

ISBN 0-8114-7230-2 (Hardcover)

ISBN 0-8114-8070-4 (Softcover)

Introduction

by Alex Haley, General Editor

It wasn't that long ago. In the days of your parents' childhood, America was a nation divided by color. Laws kept people apart, black from white. This was called segregation. Black schools, white schools. Doors closed to blacks, doors opened to whites. Restaurants, buses, trains, parks, libraries—all divided into unequal sections of black and white.

Then came the revolution that was the Civil Rights movement of the 1950's and 1960's. Many of you know the names of some of the heroes: Martin Luther King, Jr., Rosa Parks, Malcolm X. But no movement succeeds with just a few heroes making speeches or leading marches. There are many heroes or there is no success.

The story you are about to read is a story whose heroes are children like yourself. It's a story about nine African-American teenagers from Little Rock, Arkansas, who were willing to risk their lives to go to a school that they had every right to attend. Their character and courage would be tested, their determination and their dedication to the cause of justice challenged. They were nine ordinary American teenagers who volunteered to help change America.

Contents

1

Getting Ready

Wednesday, September 4, 1957, was going to be another warm, dry, sunny day in Little Rock, Arkansas. The sky was cloudless, and the temperature was already in the seventies by seven o'clock in the morning. At 4405 West 18th Street, fifteen-year-old Elizabeth Eckford was getting ready for her first day at Little Rock Central High School. The small house echoed with the morning sounds of water running in the bathroom sink and shower, doors and drawers opening and closing, and the half-awake voices of the Eckford family greeting each other good morning.

Mrs. Birdie Eckford was already in the kitchen, getting the family breakfast ready.

In the living room, Elizabeth was ironing the black-and-white dress she and her mother had made just for this day. It was hard to keep the iron moving slowly and carefully over the checkered skirt. She wanted the dress to be perfect, but her mind was racing with excitement and worry.

In just a couple of hours, she would be going to Central High, the biggest and best high school in Arkansas. Some people even said it was one of the best schools in the whole United States. Most of the students who graduated from Central went on to college. And Elizabeth certainly wanted to go to college. She'd be able to take classes at Central that weren't offered at other high schools. Going to Central would be like—well, almost like going to college itself, she thought.

But Central was an all-white school. And Elizabeth would be one of nine black students, the first of their race, to go to Central. Here was a reason to be worried.

There were plenty of whites—inside and outside the school—who didn't want any black kids going to *their* school. These people were segregationists. They believed blacks were inferior to whites and that black and white students should go to separate schools. One way or another, there would be trouble at Central. The black students would be called names, for sure. But worse things might happen.

Smelling overheated cotton, Elizabeth jerked the iron away. The last thing she wanted to do was burn the dress. Her mind had been wandering again as it had all night, keeping her awake.

Suddenly, the sound of a newscaster's voice blared through the house. Elizabeth's little brother had turned on the television. "A crowd has already gathered in front of Central High," the announcer said. "Many people wonder whether the nine Negro children will show up at Central today," he continued.

"Elizabeth, turn that thing off," Mrs. Eckford demanded from the kitchen. She wasn't excited. She was just plain worried and frightened. So was Mr. Eckford, who was walking back and forth from room to room. Mr. and Mrs. Eckford had heard enough bad news the day before—both on television and at the office of Virgil Blossom, the superintendent of schools in Little Rock.

On television Tuesday morning, they had seen pictures of Central High School surrounded by hundreds of Arkansas National Guardsmen. The guardsmen were ordered there by Arkansas Governor Orval Faubus. The governor explained that the guardsmen were there to "maintain or restore order and to protect the lives and property of citizens." He claimed that if black students attempted to go to Central, it would be impossible to maintain order. The Little Rock schools, he said, "for the time being, must be operated on the same basis as they have been operated in the past." He meant that they would stay segregated.

The only people who were not shocked by the governor's bold actions were segregationists in Little Rock and in other parts of the South. They were glad to see the governor take a stand against the Supreme Court ruling of 1954, which said that segregated schools must be integrated. They were angered that judges in Washington, D.C., were telling them how to run their schools, even though those judges served on the highest court in the nation. Governor Faubus became a hero to segregationists.

To many people in Little Rock and around the country, however, Faubus was an enemy of civil rights—the rights everyone is entitled to as a citizen of the United States. He had broken the law, and he had done so in part for selfish reasons. He wanted to be reelected governor of Arkansas, and he needed the votes of segregationists. His actions kept the black students home while white students went to their first day of school at Central.

Late Tuesday morning, Federal Judge Ronald Davies told Superintendent Blossom to go ahead with the school board's plan for integrating Central High. That afternoon, Mr. and Mrs. Eckford, the parents of the other eight teenagers, and leaders of the black community met in Mr. Blossom's office.

The big, broad-shouldered man told the parents they were to send their children to Central the next day, Wednesday. "We ask, however, that you not go with your children to Central," he said, speaking slowly and pushing his horn-rimmed glasses back on his nose. He explained that there might be a mob of white people outside Central, and the presence of the black parents might spark the mob into action. "If violence breaks out," he continued, "it will be easier to protect the children if the adults aren't there."

The parents had reason to trust what Mr. Blossom said. They knew he believed the people of the South to be law-abiding citizens. "Even though the overwhelming majority are opposed to integration," he'd said, "they will accept it because it's the law of the land."

He had worked tirelessly to set up a plan that would allow the Little Rock schools to be integrated slowly so that people could get used to the idea. His office had selected and officially accepted the nine students who would go to Central. Black leaders wanted more students, of course, but the plan and the power to make those decisions were in Mr. Blossom's hands.

No one knew, however, whether Governor Faubus would decide to obey the law and allow Central to be integrated on Wednesday, September 4. His order on the previous day had been very clear: Central was to remain segregated for the time being. The National Guardsmen had even kept Central's black adult workers away from the school that day. But Faubus now knew that Judge Davies had ordered the school board to go ahead with its integration plan. Would he change his mind and risk losing the election?

Central High had become a kind of battleground. On one side were Governor Faubus, the National Guardsmen, and the segregationists. On the other side were the Supreme Court, Judge Davies, and Mr. Blossom. The nine students were caught in the middle.

Their parents were uneasy. They were worried, fearful, and, at the same time hopeful. They worried that their teenagers might be attacked by the mob. But they knew that the law and Mr. Blossom were on their side. The time for integration had come to Little Rock, and it was a historic moment—as full of hope and promise as it was of uncertainty and danger. There seemed to be as much reason to trust that events would turn out well as there was to be worried.

The teenagers themselves were determined to go to Central. They had talked about little else since August, when school officials asked, "Who wants to go to Central? Who has good grades?" They had all raised their hands and their hopes. No one was going to keep them from going to Central now. To give up without even trying would break their hearts. And it would send the wrong message to the segregationists.

Elizabeth understood why her parents were

worried. But she was willing to risk the possible danger of a mob in order to attend Central. Her dress was ironed, and it was beautiful. It gave her a kind of courage, like a magic shield that would protect her. After breakfast, she dressed carefully, but her fingers trembled and sweated a little as she pushed the last few buttons through their holes.

Just before it was time to go, she took a final look at herself. She made sure every curl of her hair was in place. She smoothed out the skirt of her dress and made sure her petticoat was not showing. She made sure the tops of her white bobby sox were folded down exactly even with each other. She checked her spotless white canvas shoes to make sure the laces were tied tightly.

A tall, thin, attractive, rather shy brown-skinned young lady looked back at her from the mirror. Elizabeth liked what she saw and hoped everyone else would, too. Mrs. Eckford looked at Elizabeth pridefully, but she was still worried. "Don't worry, Mom," Elizabeth said, trying to reassure her.

Mr. Eckford was still pacing back and forth, looking down at the floor. Mrs. Eckford looked at her husband, then at Elizabeth. "Before you

go, Elizabeth, let's all pray," she said. For a few moments they sat together, silently holding hands in the living room. Sunlight had begun to filter through the windows. A warm breeze played with the curtains. A minute passed, then Elizabeth got up slowly, picked up her green notebook, and went out to catch the bus to Central High.

2

Turned Away

The bus rumbled and lurched down the street, heading east toward Central High. It was a short ride. Elizabeth sat calmly, a small smile on her lips. She was looking forward to seeing the other eight teenagers again. Carlotta Walls and Gloria Ray were the youngest, at fourteen. Melba Patillo, Jefferson Thomas, and Terrance Roberts were the same age as she, fifteen. Minnijean Brown, Thelma Mothershed, and Ernest Green were sixteen. They had all spent many mornings and afternoons together at Mrs. Daisy Bates's house during August.

Mrs. Bates was a leader in the black community of Little Rock. She was normally a shy, quiet woman who enjoyed gardening and making pottery. But she had a bold and strong side to her personality, too. She had learned how to fly a plane and she helped her husband run a newspaper, *The Arkansas State Press*. In their paper, they spoke out against ways that blacks in Arkansas were mistreated, especially by the white police.

Slender and only five feet three inches tall, Mrs. Bates was actually smaller than some of the teenagers. During the summer, however, she had become their coach—a tough trainer, but one who cared and listened. The teenagers needed to be ready for some of the problems they'd face at Central once school started.

Mrs. Bates helped them to understand that they had a right to go to Central. The Supreme Court had made it clear that they could not be kept from going to a school just because of the color of their skin. But once in the school, they were on their own. White students would call them names, push them, throw things at them, and try to pick fights with them. If they fought back at Central, they would surely be thrown out of the school. Mrs. Bates taught them how to stay out of fights. She helped them to learn to ignore name-calling. These were not easy things to learn. The teenagers had the same feelings as anyone else. When they were hurt, they wanted to hurt back. But there was too much at risk at Central.

Elizabeth and the other teenagers had come to regard Mrs. Bates as a second mother. They often dropped by her house on weekends just to say hello, helping themselves to sandwiches from her refrigerator. As Elizabeth rode closer to the school, she heard Mrs. Bates's voice reminding her to sit up straight, look ahead, breathe deeply, and keep calm. She squared her shoulders, lifted her head, and took a deep breath.

What Elizabeth didn't know was that while she was on her way to Central by herself, the other teenagers had gathered at Mrs. Bates's house. Late the night before, a reporter had warned Mrs. Bates of the danger the teenagers might face at Central the next day. Mrs. Bates decided to call the teenagers' parents and tell them to bring the teens to her house first thing in the morning. By going to Central as a group, they might be safer. She also called several ministers, asking them to come to her house and to walk with the students as they entered Central. She called the police, too. They said they'd meet the teens and the ministers at 12th Street, two blocks from the school. The police couldn't go any closer to Central, they said, because Governor Faubus had made the school off-limits to them.

But the Eckfords hadn't been told about this plan. They were the only family among the nine without a phone. By the time Mrs. Bates finished calling everyone else, it was almost three o'clock in the morning. Already worn out after a long day of work and worry, she decided to try to reach the Eckfords in the morning.

Wednesday morning came and eight teenagers, four ministers, and several reporters arrived. The Bateses' house hummed with activity. Amid all the business, however, Mrs. Bates forgot about the Eckfords until the other teens asked, "Where's Elizabeth?" It was already after eight o'clock, and the students had to be at Central by eight-thirty. There was no time to get to Elizabeth's house. Mr. and Mrs. Bates, the ministers, and the other teenagers left hurriedly, hoping to get to the school in time to meet Elizabeth. But it was already too late.

At 8:10, Elizabeth stepped off the bus at 17th Street and Park Street. Central was a block away, stretching from 16th to 14th streets along

Park Street. The sun was higher in the sky now. Its rays heated and brightened everything in sight. Elizabeth's eyes were sensitive, so she paused to put on her dark glasses. It was important for her to see as well as possible, and the glasses would also keep her from squinting and looking worried or afraid.

She began walking toward Central, toward 16th Street. The guardsmen were there, all right. Some sat on the curb, others stood in small groups. Still others stood in a row that went all the way around the school.

Across Park Street, a crowd of about four hundred white people stood watching the school. Reporters, photographers, and TV cameramen waited anxiously. Most of the people in the crowd were segregationists. They had come with one thing in mind—they didn't want any black students at Central. Some of the people in the crowd had come just to see the National Guardsmen—to see what was going on. After all, this was a very strange event—a high school surrounded by soldiers right in the middle of Little Rock. They sensed that something important was about to happen.

Would the guardsmen help the segregationists? Or were the soldiers "neither segregationists nor integrationists," as Governor Faubus promised? He said the guards would "protect the lives and property of citizens." Weren't black students citizens, too? They had a right to go to Central. Yet Faubus also had said "for the time being" the school should stay as it had always been—all white. Was that time over? As Elizabeth approached the school, the air was heavy with uncertainty.

Central High School had always looked a little like a castle. It was a huge yellow-brick building, shaped like a letter Y that was lying upside-down and on its side. Two parts of the five-story building spread out like wings between 14th and 16th streets. These two parts joined at the main entrance to the school. A wide double staircase led from the front lawn up to the three-door entrance.

On this day, however, Central looked like a castle at war, with armed guards surrounding the school and a mob of men, women, and teenagers swarming across the street. What Elizabeth saw caused her to slow down and come almost to a complete stop. It was as if she had unknowingly walked into a den of wild and dangerous animals—bears, rattlesnakes, tigers, and lions. Suddenly there was silence, and the crowd's eyes were all on her. Most of those eyes glowed with hatred.

It was too late to turn back, even though that's what she felt like doing. She would have liked to disappear into thin air, too, but that was impossible. All those people! All those hateful eyes! And not another black face to be seen. Where were the other eight teenagers?

Somehow she kept her feet moving, but her fingers gripped her notebook tightly. She clenched her jaw. Her breath became shallow. She had no choice now but to believe the guardsmen would protect her.

She thought it would be safe to walk on the sidewalk behind the row of guards. That way the guards would be between her and the crowd. She could see the sidewalk leading down the block to the main entrance.

Crossing the street, she came up to one guard. She looked at him hopefully and even tried to shape her mouth into a little smile. The guard stood straight and tall. The butt end of his rifle rested on the ground, its muzzle held firmly in his right hand. To Elizabeth, he seemed much taller because he was standing on the curb and she was standing in the street. He did not look at her. Instead he pointed across the street.

Elizabeth looked across the street, not quite sure what to do. But she felt she had to trust the guard. There was no one else to guide her. She wanted to go into Central High, and he knew the way. She would follow his instructions. "You mean I should walk over there and down the street?" she asked.

The silent guard nodded.

She walked across the street, away from the guards and toward the crowd. A soft breeze tickled the leaves of the big oak trees lining Park Street. That was the only sound. Then, as Elizabeth got closer to the curb, she heard feet shuffling. The crowd was moving back, away from her, as if to make room for her.

"Here she comes. Get ready!" yelled someone. Without thinking, Elizabeth stepped back. She could feel the danger. She had gone too close to them. She needed to walk more in the center of the street. That way, if the crowd got too close, she could walk closer to the guards and they'd protect her. She still felt the confidence she'd gotten from talking to the guard. But it didn't last long.

Walking down the middle of Park Street now, she saw the crowd start to follow her. They started hooting, sneering, and yelling names at her. Her knees began to shake. Yes, the guards were there, but would she make it to the entrance? Her fingers began to sweat. They gripped her notebook tighter still. A knot of fear began to tighten in her stomach.

Near the entrance to the school, some white students were passing through the line of guards. There it is, she thought. That's the way in. She walked to where the other students went through the line. The crowd stopped yelling. There was silence again, except for the chatter of some of the white students who'd passed through the line of guards. This was the moment the crowd had been waiting for. Were the guards going to let her through or were they going to turn her away?

Elizabeth tried to step up on the curb and go past a guardsman. But the guard didn't move to let her through. She tried again. This time, the guard raised his rifle and kept her from squeezing past him. Two other guards raised their rifles and moved to keep her from going through. The guards were not protecting her, after all. They were turning her away from the school and back to the angry crowd—back to the mob.

Elizabeth turned around, and there they were. Their hateful eyes stared at her. The guards were on their side, after all. "Lynch her! Lynch her!" someone shouted. They were mad enough to kill her.

Every muscle of her body became stiff. She shook with terror. She could hardly breathe. It was as if her body wanted to turn into a rock that human hands couldn't hurt. But she was not a rock. She was a human being. She could be hurt. She could bleed. She could be killed. And, at that moment, it seemed there was no one to protect her.

From the mob, a hand reached out to grab her. Quickly, a guard stepped forward and pushed the person back. Were the guards protecting her after all? Why wouldn't they let her in the school, then? No one said anything to her that made her feel safe. All she heard were hateful shouts and jeers from the mob. In panic, she searched the mob for a face that would give her that sense of safety. One pair of soft, friendly, or even worried eyes—that's all she wanted. One woman looked nice. But when Elizabeth looked at her again to make sure, the woman spit in her face.

She looked down the block and saw another bus stop. She thought if she could get there, she'd be all right. Maybe it looked safe to her

because there was no one there. Maybe it was because there was a bench there and she could sit down and collect her thoughts. Whatever the reason, it looked like the place to go.

It wasn't far away, but getting there turned out to be one of the longest walks in her life. She was surrounded by white people. Reporters, photographers, and men with television cameras scrambled in front of her. The mob was behind her.

"No nigger is going to get in our school," shouted someone in the mob. "Get out of here!" yelled someone else.

Out of the corner of her eye, she saw the guards along the sidewalk. The blank, empty looks on their faces told her she couldn't count on them now. She was alone and terrified. They had all let her down—the guards, Mrs. Bates, the other teenagers. It was the worst thing that could happen to her. It took every bit of courage she had to reach the bus stop. She walked slowly, looking straight ahead, trying to ignore the threats and shouts. She wasn't sure she'd make it alive.

Finally, she reached the bench at the bus stop. But there was no bus. She'd have to wait.

But for how long? Would the mob attack her? She sat as still as a stone. She was so frightened that she couldn't move. The mob had drawn closer around her. "Drag her over to that tree," a voice screamed. "Let's get her." She felt as if she were trapped in a living nightmare. She couldn't talk, she couldn't scream, she couldn't run.

A reporter shoved a microphone in her face and began asking questions. "Can you tell me your name?" he asked.

She was frozen with fear. She couldn't open her mouth. She felt that if she tried to speak, all the terror she felt would show in her voice. Then everyone would know she was afraid, and it would be worse.

"Are you going to go to school here at Central High today?" he asked.

Elizabeth was silent.

"You don't care to tell me anything, is that right?" he asked.

She stared straight ahead. The longer she waited for the bus, the more unreal things seemed. All she wanted was to be out of there, out of danger, and safely at home. The reporter turned toward a television camera and began to describe what was happening. He moved away, and Elizabeth was alone again on the bench with the mob around her. She lowered her head. Tears began to fall from under her dark glasses. Quickly and quietly, another reporter sat down next to her. "I'm a reporter from *The New York Times*," he said. "May I have your name?" Still terrified, Elizabeth said nothing. Seeing how frightened she was, the reporter put his arm around her. He lifted her chin. "Don't let them see you cry," he said softly. This made her feel a little better. At least there was one person who tried to help her. But she was still frightened. This was only one man. There were hundreds of angry people around her. Besides, the mob was now yelling at the reporter, too. He might not be any safer than she was.

The mob was drawing the attention of passersby who wanted to know what was going on. One of these people was Mrs. Grace Lorch, who just happened to be driving by when she heard the noise. Mrs. Lorch's husband taught at a black college in Little Rock. She knew how dangerous some of the segregationists could be. She parked her car where it was and ran toward the mob. She saw how they were terrorizing Elizabeth.

Pushing her way through the mob, she yelled, "Leave this child alone! Why are you tormenting her?"

"What are you doing, you nigger lover?" someone in the mob screamed back. "You stay away from that girl."

Mrs. Lorch looked at Elizabeth, then looked at the mob again. "You can see she's in a state of shock," she said urgently. "Someone has to help her." She tried to get the mob to back off. "Why don't you calm down?" she asked. "I'm not here to fight with you. Six months from now you'll be ashamed of what you're doing."

But the mob wouldn't listen. "Go home. You're just one of them," a voice shouted.

Mrs. Lorch walked Elizabeth across the street to a drugstore. She wanted to call a taxi and get Elizabeth home. They were about to enter the store when someone inside angrily slammed the door shut in their face.

At that moment, Elizabeth saw the bus coming. She and Mrs. Lorch walked quickly toward it. Some people from the mob were still following them, shouting angry words. The bus was slowed down by traffic that had been jammed by the mob. Elizabeth and Mrs. Lorch got on the bus even before it reached the stop. As the doors closed on the bus, the few members of the mob who had run after Elizabeth and Mrs. Lorch trotted to a halt and turned back. In a short time, Elizabeth was safely home.

Meanwhile, on their way to Central, Mrs. Bates and her husband turned on the car radio. They heard a news flash that a black girl was being attacked by a mob in front of the school. "Oh, my God," gasped Mrs. Bates. "It's Elizabeth."

Mr. Bates raced the car as close to the school as he could get. He and Mrs. Bates ran in the direction of the mob, but by the time they got there, Elizabeth had gone.

Just minutes later, the other black teenagers and the ministers arrived.

When the other teenagers tried to enter Central, they too were met with raised rifles that kept them out. They were also yelled at by the mob. Sensing the danger, the ministers quickly guided the teens back to the cars and drove them home. It was clear that the guards were not going to let them in the school. What would the next step be?

3

Day One—In and Out, Quick

On Friday, September 20, Judge Davies ruled that Governor Faubus had indeed disobeyed the Supreme Court order that schools be integrated. The judge ordered the governor to stop using the National Guard to keep the students out of Central.

On television that night, Governor Faubus gave his response to the judge's order. Looking very businesslike in his dark suit, white shirt, and dark tie, he said, "I have tried to follow a course that would preserve and maintain the peace and order in Little Rock and in the state." He continued in a steady, calm voice that barely masked his anger. "Now that a Federal court, however, has chosen to substitute its judgment for mine as to how the peace and order should be preserved, I must temporarily at least abide. Therefore I have issued orders that all units of the Arkansas National Guard stationed in Little Rock be removed."

Winding up his speech, he asked that black students voluntarily stay away from Central "until such time as there is assurance that [their right to integrate] can be accomplished in a peaceful manner." The governor did not say how much time this would take.

Mrs. Bates was not fooled by the governor's words. She knew that if it were left to him, black students would never be allowed into Central. She wasn't going to wait.

"These students are definitely going to enter Central High School," she said. "They have been enrolled and officially accepted. That is the only school open to them now." She was just not sure if they would enter the next Monday, or a day or two later.

Since the ugly run-in with the mob on September 4, Mrs. Bates and the students had been busy. First had come a difficult peacemaking between Elizabeth and Mrs. Bates.

After facing the mob, Elizabeth had become a kind of heroine. Pictures of her appeared in newspapers everywhere. Reporters wanted to talk to her, but her parents would not allow it for several days. She was not a happy heroine. She needed a rest. Nightmares disturbed her sleep every night. She woke up terrified and screaming. And she still blamed Mrs. Bates for having to face the mob alone. She and her family felt betrayed and had refused to speak to Mrs. Bates for days.

Finally, Elizabeth agreed to go to Mrs. Bates's to talk to reporters. She rang the bell and Mrs. Bates answered. It was the first time they had seen each other in more than a week. It was an awkward moment. Mrs. Bates smiled warmly and invited Elizabeth in, but her eyes showed that she still felt guilty because she hadn't found a way to warn the Eckfords about the plan.

Elizabeth was very quiet. She said hardly anything, and her eyes avoided those of Mrs. Bates. Knowing something was wrong, the older woman asked Elizabeth to come into the bedroom first before talking to the reporters. "How are you feeling now?" she asked.

Elizabeth spun around and glared at Mrs. Bates. Her eyes were filled with anger, hurt, and tears. "Why am I here?" she demanded. "Why are you so interested in how I feel *now*? You didn't care enough to tell me about the change in plans."

Elizabeth's bitter words made Mrs. Bates feel helpless and sad. The woman had made a terrible mistake, but it had not been on purpose. How could she make Elizabeth understand? She began to explain.

Sobbing, Elizabeth listened as Mrs. Bates described what had happened. Expressing her anger at Mrs. Bates had helped ease some of the pain she felt. Hearing Mrs. Bates's gentle, anguished voice made her realize how much she and the other teenagers needed this courageous woman's help. But it took a couple of days before she could fully forgive Mrs. Bates.

After their talk, Elizabeth returned to the living room, followed by Mrs. Bates, and answered the reporters' questions as well as she could. It wasn't easy. The frightful experience with the mob was still fresh in her mind, and her nerves were still raw. By the end of the interview, however, she had impressed the reporters with her quiet dignity and maturity.

For the next few days, Elizabeth joined the eight other students in a study group. They called the principal at Central, Mr. Jess Matthews, and asked for assignments. Mrs. Bates arranged for them to be tutored by teachers from a nearby college.

They worked hard at their lessons, but it was not the same as being at Central. Even though they were all good students, they knew they'd have to work hard to make good grades at Central. It was a tough school, and the longer they had to stay away, the harder it would be to catch up. The news that Governor Faubus had removed the National Guard was a big boost to their spirits. It was a kind of victory. But there were many questions still to be answered.

■ ■ ■ ■ ■ ■

On Sunday afternoon, September 22, Elizabeth came to visit Mrs. Bates. She sat on the curved sectional sofa in Mrs. Bates's living room. "Now that the National Guard's gone, what's going to happen?" she asked. "Are we going in tomorrow? Will we have protection this time?"

Elizabeth's tone of voice conveyed both her worry and her determination. She had already been through one horrible situation alone. She wasn't going to let that happen again. She was asking the questions that needed to be asked. She wasn't angry at Mrs. Bates now, but she wanted to know the facts.

Mrs. Bates started to answer, but caught herself before the words got out. The memory of the mistake that had let Elizabeth face the mob alone flashed through her mind. Her reply would have to reassure Elizabeth that it would be safe to go to Central. At the same time, however, she couldn't guarantee there'd be no further danger.

Taking a breath, she sat next to Elizabeth and put her arm around the girl. "I'm sure you'll have protection," she said, gently hugging her. "Marvin Potts, the Chief of Police, is putting the Little Rock police forces on alert," she continued. "And the school board is meeting this afternoon. Later today I should know when you'll be going to school and what kind of protection you'll get."

Late Sunday night, Superintendent Blossom called Mrs. Bates. He told her to have the students at her house early Monday morning.

"Tomorrow morning, you'll get more information about how the children will get to school," he said. "The city police will be at the school," he assured her.

His words made her feel more confident. It sounded as if the school board and the police had worked out a plan for protecting the students, and she believed that they would abide by the law and by Judge Davies's ruling against Governor Faubus. There would be a mob—she knew that. (They had gathered outside Central every school day for two weeks after the students were turned away the first time.) But the mob wouldn't have the National Guard to back up its effort to keep the teens out of Central.

The nine teenagers and their parents were at Mrs. Bates's house by eight o'clock Monday morning. After leaving their teens with Mrs. Bates, all but two of the parents left for work. Mr. Eckford and Mrs. Brown stayed on to drive the students to school.

Reporters and photographers had arrived at Mrs. Bates's house, too. The story of the "Little Rock Nine," as they'd come to be called, had grabbed the attention of the country and of many parts of the world. It was a big story. Little Rock was still part of the "Old South," where segregation had been in force since slavery times.

Little Rock had made some changes to weaken segregation. Black and white families lived next door to each other in some parts of the city. The city's buses were integrated. But the schools were among the last strongholds of segregation in Little Rock. Reporters, photographers, and television crews were there to record how this part of the battle would be played out. Outside of Central High School, hundreds of segregationists waited, along with more reporters and photographers.

"Do you think the black students will get in today?" a reporter asked one of them, a big man in overalls.

"They're not going to get in," the man snarled. "They won't live long enough to get to the doors."

"We won't stand for our schools being integrated," huffed someone else.

Mrs. Bates, the students, and the two parents heard these and other comments on the radio as they waited. Nobody said anything, but the air in the Bateses' living room was thick with anger, worry, and determination.

Elizabeth sat alone. Once again, she became frozen with fear. Of all the people in that room, she alone knew what it was like to face the full fury of a mob. The voices on the radio stirred her terror-stricken memory of the voices she'd heard eighteen days before outside Central.

Carlotta Walls and Ernest Green paced nervously from one room to another. They knew it would be rough, but they wanted to get started. Waiting only made them more nervous.

Mrs. Brown sat on the sofa where Elizabeth had sat the day before. Her eyes were closed, her hands were pressed tightly together, and she prayed silently. Mr. Eckford sat across the room from her. His head was also bowed in prayer. This was torture for him. Once again, it seemed to him, his daughter's life would be in danger. She had had a close call once. Would she be so lucky a second time?

The sharp jangle of the telephone startled everyone. It was a police officer. "Don't take the usual route to school," he said. "It's best if you go a different way. We'll meet you near the 16th Street entrance to Central and take the students in by the side door."

Meanwhile, two blocks from the school, three black reporters and a black photographer got out of a car. Intending to report on the events of the day, they began walking toward the school. At about eight forty-five they reached Park Street and came face to face with a mob of about a hundred whites.

The mob surged toward the men, shouting, "Here come the niggers." One man in the mob growled, "We're not going to let you niggers pass. This is our school. Go back where you came from." Their faces were twisted and red with rage. One of the reporters, James Hicks, raised the palms of both hands toward the mob. "We're not trying to go to school," he explained calmly. "We're reporters."

"We don't care," shouted the mob leader, his fists clenched as he spat out his words. "You're niggers and we're not going to let you go any further."

Then someone yelled, "Kill 'em!" and the mob began chasing the men. They tripped, beat, and kicked the reporters. They hit one reporter in the head with a brick. They smashed the photographer's camera. In a frantic scramble, the men outran the mob and escaped with their lives.

Meanwhile, the nine students had slipped through a side entrance of Central High. The mob's attention had been on the black reporters, not on the school. It hadn't been planned that way, but the mob's hatred had distracted them from their goal.

Inside the school, the students were met by Craig Raines, an officer of the student council. Like many of the white students, he was not in favor of integration, either. He too thought it should be the right of people in Arkansas to decide, not the Supreme Court or the government in Washington. But three weeks ago, as he raised the flag outside Central, he had seen Elizabeth being terrorized by the mob. He was shocked and ashamed that white people would act that way. What he saw that day helped him begin to change his mind about going to school with black students.

Craig took the students to meet the principal, Mr. Matthews. At Mr. Matthews's office they got their class schedules, then set out to find their way to their classes.

Each of them was in a different homeroom, and no two students were in the same class together except for the girls who were paired for gym class. Some were in different grades, of course. But it seemed to them as if they had been deliberately separated by the school officials. Was it so that they would not attract so much attention? Was it so that they could not talk to each other or protect each other? They didn't know. All they knew was that each of them would be alone much of the time in a huge school with 1,500 white students.

They had been told that they might be hit, kicked, and called names by students inside Central. Would it really happen, they wondered nervously as they went to their classes.

Melba Patillo had to take the stairs from the first floor to the third floor. As she walked, she looked neither to the right nor to the left. She looked down at her feet and kept walking and climbing and saying a prayer to herself, hoping to be left alone. No one bothered her. She breathed easier as she found her seat in her first class. Then, as the class began, she heard loud roaring outside the school. Sounds like a football game, she thought. But she knew it wasn't a football game. The roaring was too angry for that. The mob had learned that the nine students were inside the school, and the news made them furious.

"Let's go!" someone in the mob shouted. They were going to try to enter Central to get the students. They began pushing against the wooden barriers that kept them from the school.

The Little Rock police fought back with nightsticks, but the mob was getting stronger.

Inside Central, several white students walked out of their classes. They didn't want to go to school with black students. A white girl, on her way out, slapped Melba's face. "Thank you," Melba said, remembering some of the lessons she'd learned from Mrs. Bates. "I can take that, too." It was the hardest thing Melba had ever had to say. But she knew she could not hit back.

Most of the white students, however, were better behaved than the girl who slapped Melba. Some were openly friendly and kind to the black students. In music class, Minnijean Brown tried out her voice. After hearing her sing, one white student said, "Oh, you're so good!" Others joined in with compliments. They made her feel just like a regular student. In the hall, another white girl ran up to her and said, "I'm so glad you're here. Won't you go to lunch with me today?"

A few minutes before noon, a monitor from the principal's office came into Ernest Green's science class. "You have to go to the principal's office right away," the monitor said.

When Ernest got there, he saw the other eight students. They looked scared. Several official-looking white people were standing around. They looked tense and worried. Mr. Matthews began speaking. "The police chief, Mr. Smith, has requested that you be sent home. He's worried about your safety."

Central was indeed not safe for the students at that moment. Several white parents had entered the school and had taken their children out. The mob outside the school was getting out of control. Soon the police would be unable to hold them back. Some police officers had even taken off their badges, thrown them to the ground, and joined the mob.

How could the nine students get out of the school safely? One official was heard to say, "If we allow the mob to hang one kid, then we might be able to get the rest out while they're hanging that kid." The teenagers couldn't believe their ears.

Angered by the brutality of the suggestion, another official said with disgusted irony, "But how are you going to choose? You're going to let them draw straws?"

This was no joke to the students. They'd all heard stories about black people who had been lynched by mobs. And now they were surrounded by white people, with an angry mob ready to tear the school apart just to get its hands on them.

Finally, Police Chief Smith said, "I'll get them out." He led the students down a dark stairway to the school delivery entrance in the basement. Two plain blue-gray cars were parked there. Helping the students get into the cars, Chief Smith spoke to the drivers. "Once you start driving," he warned, "don't stop." Then the entrance doors opened, and the cars roared out.

From inside the locked cars, the teenagers saw hands grabbing at the door handles and tail fins of the cars. They saw fists beating on the wraparound windows. They heard angry screaming and yelling. They saw that some of the whites had guns.

But the drivers followed Chief Smith's orders. The cars charged through the mob, causing the people to scatter to the sides of the road.

After escaping the mob, the drivers took each student home. As Melba got out, she turned to the driver and said, "Thanks for the ride." Later, she realized she should have said, "Thanks for my life."

4

A Little Help from the President

As the sun set on that dry, hot September day, gangs of angry whites rioted through Little Rock. They attacked and beat black people. They smashed car windows. Other white people made threatening calls to the homes of black families and to the white parents whose children had been kind to the nine students.

Police were ordered to guard the homes of the nine students, and a squad car was parked across the street from Mrs. Bates's house, too. This was not the first time her house needed protection. One night in August, a rock had come crashing through the picture window in the living room. Attached to the rock was a note that said, "Stone this time, dynamite next." At another time, a firebomb was thrown into her carport, and crosses were burned on the lawn.

Mrs. Bates, her husband, and a few reporters now sat in the darkened house. They watched for strange cars and listened for strange sounds.

Soon, a car cruised by slowly with its lights off. The police car began to follow it. Less than an hour later, there was a knock on the Bateses' front door. Mr. Bates saw that it was a policeman. Turning on a light, he unlocked and opened the door.

"Turn off that light," hissed the policeman, stepping inside quickly. "And stay away from the window." Mr. and Mrs. Bates could tell there was trouble.

"We just stopped a motorcade of about a hundred cars, two blocks from here," the policeman said, almost breathless and swallowing hard. "When we followed the car that passed, we ran into the mob head-on. We radioed for help, and a whole group of city and Federal agents showed up. We found dynamite, guns, pistols, clubs—everything—in the cars. Some of the mob got away on foot, leaving their cars. We don't know what will happen tonight, so no one is to leave the house."

No one did. And no one slept, either.

The news from Little Rock shocked people around the country and in other parts of the world. But more shocks were yet to come. The mob was not going to give up easily.

■ ■ ■ ■ ■ ■

In Washington, D.C., President Eisenhower was growing more and more irritated with the situation in Little Rock. Since its beginning, he'd hoped Governor Faubus would obey the Supreme Court order and prove to be a leader in helping integration occur peacefully in the South. He'd even met with the governor, who had promised that he'd tell the National Guard to protect the nine teenagers as they entered Central. Instead, Faubus had ordered the guardsmen to leave Central altogether. Then he went off to a conference in Georgia, allowing the mob to riot freely and take control of Little Rock. President Eisenhower was furious.

The evening of September 23, as the mob began attacking people, President Eisenhower decided it was necessary to get tough. He issued an executive order calling for everyone who was preventing the students from entering and remaining in Central to "cease and desist."

"I will use the full power of the United States," he warned, "to prevent any obstruction of the law and carry out the orders of the Federal Court."

Mrs. Bates heard the President's order, but she didn't think the order by itself was enough protection for the teenagers. She told them to stay home the next day, Tuesday, September 24.

She did the right thing. On Tuesday morning, a mob of about five hundred people gathered again in front of the school. They paid no attention to President Eisenhower's order. In their minds, the President of the United States had no right to tell the state of Arkansas what to do. As citizens of Arkansas, they didn't want integration and they weren't going to allow it. They remained outside the school until it was clear that the teenagers weren't showing up.

Late that afternoon, as dusk began to settle, the air around Little Rock filled with a great rumbling sound. It was not thunder—there hadn't been much rain at all during September. No, this was the rumble of big airplanes landing at the Air Force base in Little Rock.

The planes carried a thousand soldiers of the 101st Airborne Division. Top soldiers, trained for battle, arrived from Fort Campbell, Kentucky. President Eisenhower had ordered them to go to Little Rock and make sure the nine students went to Central High School safely.

The President was showing the mob he meant business.

"Come on, Mrs. Bates," a reporter called to her as he was leaving her house. "Aren't you going to see the troops enter the city?"

"No," she replied. "But thank God they're here."

Moments later, however, Mrs. Bates did go out into her front yard. She saw her neighbors standing and looking at the sky. It had been a long time since she or her neighbors had stood outdoors without fear. She listened a while longer to the delicious sounds of the planes, which were now joined by the sounds of children laughing as they played outdoors. Then she went back inside to wait for a call from Mr. Blossom. She expected him to tell her when the students could come back to Central.

During the evening, long lines of jeeps and trucks carried the soldiers into town. The soldiers were dressed in full combat gear—boots, helmets, canteens, handguns strapped to their waists—carrying rifles with bayonets. Some had nightsticks, too. The dusky air around Central was now filled with the roar of jeep and truck engines, the squawking of walkie-talkies, the thudding of heavy combat boots, and the rattle of military equipment.

The soldiers parked the gray-green vehicles in front of the school and on the school playing fields. By 10:00 P.M., Central looked more like an Army fort than a high school.

Earlier that evening, President Eisenhower appeared on television. He said he'd sent the soldiers to Little Rock "solely for the purpose of preventing interference with the order of the Court."

"I know that the . . . majority of the people in the South—including those of Arkansas and of Little Rock—are of good will," the President said. He said he believed the people were "united in their efforts to preserve and respect the law even if they disagree with it." And he reminded the people that "respect for law" was the basis for the American way of life.

Just before midnight, Mrs. Bates got a call from Mr. Blossom. He said he'd heard that she told the students to stay home Wednesday.

"That's correct," Mrs. Bates said.

"But the commander of the troops, General Walker, said he's here to put the children in school," Mr. Blossom said in alarm. "So you must have them at your house by eight-thirty in the morning."

"I can't," Mrs. Bates replied curtly. She was getting annoyed with these last-minute orders. "I can't reach them. We have an agreement that if I want them, I will call *before* midnight," she continued. "In order to get some sleep and avoid the harrassing calls, they take their phones off the hook after midnight."

It had been a long day, and Mrs. Bates was tired and irritated. But she knew this was an important opportunity. Her tone softened. "I suppose I could go to each home," she said. "But I can't go alone."

Mr. Blossom said he'd ask the principals of the two black high schools to go with her. And they did. For the next three hours—the first dark morning hours of Wednesday, September 25—Mrs. Bates and the two principals went around to the nine black students' homes. They told the parents to have the students at Mrs. Bates's house by 8:30 that morning.

By 8:35, all nine students, along with several reporters, were at Mrs. Bates's house. They were excited and anxious. The reporters asked questions, but the teenagers found it hard to talk.

The ring of the telephone put an end to the question-and-answer session. Mrs. Bates answered. It was someone from the office at Central.

"Are the children all there?" the person asked.

"All nine," said Mrs. Bates.

"Well, the soldiers are on their way to pick them up," the school official said.

About a half hour later, a gray-green station wagon and several jeeps filled with soldiers came to a stop in front of Mrs. Bates's house. Jefferson Thomas was the first to see them. "The Army's here! They're here!" he shouted.

The reporters ran out of the house and scrambled to places where they could see and take pictures. The soldiers hopped out of the jeeps and stood at attention at opposite ends of the street.

The paratroop leader got out of the station wagon and walked toward the house. Minnijean saw him approach. "Oh, look at them, they're so—so soldierly," she said joyfully. "It gives you goose pimples to look at them." Turning to look at Mrs. Bates, she said proudly, "For the first time in my life, I feel like an American citizen."

The paratrooper rang the doorbell. Opening the door, Mrs. Bates saw a tall, combat-ready

soldier standing at attention and saluting her. "Mrs. Bates, we're ready for the children. We will return them to your home at three-thirty o'clock."

With that, the nine students followed him to the station wagon. The girls, some of them wearing crisp, pressed, brightly colored dresses, sat in the front and rear seats. The three boys, wearing short-sleeved shirts and jeans with wide cuffs, climbed into the back end.

A jeep pulled up in front of the car. Four paratroopers jumped in and sat down, holding their rifles by their sides, their bayonets pointing skyward. Another jeep pulled up behind, and four more soldiers took their positions inside it.

Looking out the back of the station wagon, Ernest noticed the machine-gun mounts on the jeep behind him. The soldiers sat stiff and action-ready. Their green helmets seemed to give off a dim glow in the morning sunlight. As the caravan pulled away from the curb and headed toward Central, Ernest turned to Terrance and said, "I guess we're going to get into school today."

5

First Full Day

School had begun as usual for most of the white students at Central. At 8:45, the United States flag was raised. The bugle sounded the "call to colors," and the students and teachers placed their right hands over their hearts and recited the Pledge of Allegiance. But everyone knew this was not just another morning at Central High School.

At a nine o'clock assembly, General Edwin A. Walker, the commander of the soldiers, spoke to the white students. He explained the 1954 Supreme Court decision—that skin color could no longer be the reason for sending children to separate schools. The President had ordered the

Army and the National Guard to carry out the Court's orders, he said. "As an officer of the United States Army," he announced, "I have been chosen to command these forces and to execute the President's orders."

The tall, no-nonsense commander recognized the audience as "law-abiding citizens," and said they had nothing to fear. However, he warned that "Those who interfere or disrupt the proper administration of the school will be removed by the soldiers . . . and turned over to the local police."

While General Walker spoke, a mob gathered across the street from the school. It was much smaller than the previous day's mob but just as angry and stubborn. They ignored Major James Morris's orders to go home, so Major Morris radioed for help. Within minutes, a squad of soldiers arrived and moved steadily toward the mob, bayonets lowered and pointing straight ahead.

The mob jeered at the soldiers, but then began to back away, just a step ahead of the bayonets. In a few moments, the mob broke up as the white people went away in separate directions. Park Street was now clear except for a few Army vehicles. But the calm was only temporary. Minutes after the mob broke up, about eighty students stormed out of Central. They were segregationists who had heard General Walker's speech. Rather than stay around when the nine students entered, they decided to leave. They tramped across Park Street and spread out along the sidewalk in front of the houses facing Central.

At 9:22, the Army convoy carrying the nine students drew up in front of the school. Soldiers in front of the school snapped to attention. The troops in the jeeps in front of and behind the station wagon jumped out and stood at attention, too. Then the students got out. The soft fabrics and bright colors of their clothes stood out like dazzling sails against the soldiers' drab green uniforms and hard helmets. Still more soldiers double-timed forward to surround and protect the students. Then, in one large group, the soldiers and students walked up the wide front staircase to Central High's main entrance.

As they walked up the stairs, the nine teenagers were full of pride and a sense of victory. After all, the President of the United States had sent in the paratroopers to escort them to school! This meant that they really were citizens of the United States. It meant the United

States stood behind its promise of liberty and justice for all. It was a moment none of them would ever forget.

From across the street, the white students shouted, "Two, four, six, eight, we ain't gonna integrate." But their jeers were mostly drowned out by the loud flutter of an Army helicopter hovering watchfully above the entrance.

As the nine students walked through the doorway, they were greeted by Mr. Matthews. "Well, good morning, boys and girls," he said. "This is the first class period, and you all know your way to that class. You may go to class, now."

Each student headed to a different class, followed by his or her own personal soldier. During the day, the soldiers stood outside the classrooms. When classes changed, they walked with the students to the next class. The soldiers didn't baby the students. They were polite, they paid attention to the students, but they also did their job—they watched for trouble and they made the students feel safe.

The first full day at Central was surprisingly trouble free. Most of the segregationist students had left after General Walker's speech or had not come to school that day at all. But before

noon, the principal's office received two calls warning that a bomb was going to explode in the school. Mr. Matthews decided to have a fire drill to get the students out of the school.

In no time at all, about 1,000 students filed out of Central and joined 350 soldiers standing outside. (Not all of the 1,000 soldiers were on duty at once, and some of them had been sent to guard other parts of Little Rock.) Photographers and reporters jockeyed to get pictures and ask questions. The fire drill added to the excitement and nervous tension of the day. Many students laughed and giggled, while others were quiet and sulky.

A reporter spotted Minnijean talking with a blonde classmate. "Are you making any friends?" he asked.

"Yes I am," she replied, smiling. "Quite a few, indeed."

"We'd work this thing out for ourselves," said a white senior, "if the parents would just go home and leave us be."

Another senior commented, "It's just the idea of going to school with colored kids that's hard to take at first. Once you get used to the idea, it's not bad."

It was a new experience for everyone. Black families and white families lived next door to each other in some parts of Little Rock. But black students and white students had never gone to the same public school in the city before. Some white students didn't mind integration, but others were bitter.

"I'm not going to school with niggers," said one boy who had walked out of Central earlier. "If I catch one, I'll chase him out of school," he continued. His sixteen-year-old sister remarked, "If they didn't have soldiers in the halls, the niggers would get murdered."

Very few other students agreed with her. During the rest of the day, white students helped black students find their classes. White students and black students had lunch together. In Melba Patillo's third-period gym class, white girls asked her to join their baseball team. Melba hit two home runs.

School was over at 3:00 P.M. The nine students were met by the soldiers at a side entrance. As another helicopter hovered overhead, the students climbed into the station wagon. Paratroopers hopped into the two jeeps, and the convoy sped away, returning the students to Mrs. Bates's house.

Mrs. Bates was relieved to see the students safe again. She had worried all day about what was happening to them. Now she was eager to hear how the day had gone. "Did you have a rough day?" she asked, after they'd all settled down.

"Not especially," one teenager said a little sourly.

"So-so," said another with a shrug.

"Not too bad," another said half-heartedly.

"I was invited to join the glee club," Minnijean said casually, as if she really didn't care.

The students were acting rather strangely. This had been a day of victory. They had finally spent a full day at Central and had returned safely. Yet no one seemed very excited now that it was over.

Mrs. Bates was confused and concerned. Her smile turned to a worried frown. "Why the long faces?" she asked.

"Well," Ernest began, "you don't expect us to be jumping for joy, do you?" He looked annoyed.

One of the girls said, "But Ernest, we *are* in Central, and that shouldn't make us feel sad exactly."

"Sure we're in Central," Ernest shot back.

"But how did we get in? We got in, finally, because we were protected by paratroops. Some victory!"

"Are you sorry that the President sent the troops?" one of the boys asked.

"No," replied Ernest, looking down at the floor. "I'm only sorry it had to be that way."

So the day's victory was not total, after all. The students realized that afternoon at Mrs. Bates's that they still faced a powerful enemy. That enemy was racism—the belief that black people are inferior and should be treated unfairly. They wondered how long they would have to go to school under the protection of soldiers. And what would happen if the soldiers were called off?

Later that afternoon, the teenagers' parents came to pick them up from Mrs. Bates's house. In the evening, there was homework for everyone. But Melba also found time to write a story about her first full day at school. Her story appeared the next day on the front page of the *New York Post*. Here's part of what she wrote.

Where were you about 9:15 yesterday morning? I was just discovering a wonderful

America, an America with freedom and justice for all.

I did not know what to do as I arose yesterday morning. I had prayed to the utmost of my ability but I still had doubts. Then suddenly it hit me: I must go to Central High again.

My heart ached Monday after having been taken from Central H.S. I wondered just how does this system of law we have work.

Previous to Monday I thought that a few people could not decide against something, against an issue, and thus make a law ineffective. But to my astonishment it had happened. Not calmly or quietly, but with all the thunder of a falling mountain.

But that great thunder came to an end this morning, for I, Melba Patillo, a Negro, had the pride, pleasure and honor of seeing this great America with her democracy in action. Just seeing the paratroopers and being escorted into Central H.S. gave me a feeling which I never experienced before. I shall never experience it again. . . .

After I had entered the halls of Central my day became that of most any other child. . . . I'm as pleased as could be about the day, for I was treated as well as could be expected under the circumstances.

A great part of the student body was absent. I have no way of knowing what they will do or say when they return with their prejudices. All I can do is hope for the best.

The few children who were nice today helped my outlook on life tremendously. Little things do mean a lot.

—From the *New York Post*, Thursday, September 26, 1957. Reprinted with permission.

6

A Declaration of War—and a Final Victory

During the school year, Melba would be forced to change her rosy attitude about Central High School.

The paratroopers did their job—the nine students were in Central and no mob tried to keep them out after September 25. A week later, half the paratroopers left Central. They were replaced by a much smaller group of the Arkansas National Guard who were under President Eisenhower's orders, not Governor Faubus's. But the Arkansas guards had a different attitude toward the nine teenagers. They were not as watchful or as protective as the paratroopers had been.

The nine students were not sure why the guards behaved differently. Perhaps the guards were segregationists themselves and were bitter at having to protect the students rather than turn them away from Central. Perhaps it was that the National Guardsmen were not as well trained as the paratroopers. Maybe they didn't take their job as seriously as the paratroopers had. Whatever the reason, the Little Rock Nine began to feel less safe after the paratroopers left.

The white students who were absent or who walked out on September 25 drifted back into Central. About fifty of these students were out-and-out segregationists. With the help of adults outside the school, they plotted to get rid of the nine students. Their plan was to attack the teenagers in small ways every day until the black students gave up or got in trouble by fighting back and were then expelled.

The white students weren't afraid of being caught or reported to the office. They too sensed that the guards in the halls, the National Guardsmen, were not as protective as the paratroopers. And there were plenty of chances to attack in the student bathrooms and in the gym where the guards were not allowed to go. Excuses would be easy to make up. Everybody knows how rough teens can be with each other—just "kids' play." And everybody knows that accidents can happen. . . . "Oops, sorry, I didn't see you."

So the attacks began. Day after day, Melba, Minnijean, Thelma, Gloria, Carlotta, Elizabeth, Terrance, Ernest, and Jefferson were kicked, tripped, knocked down, shoved against lockers, and called names. Their lockers were broken into and their books stolen or ripped up. The whites threw sharpened pencils, spitballs, and wads of paper at them. They squirted ink on the girls' clothes.

In gym class, Melba was pushed down onto a broken bottle on the pavement. Acid was thrown at her, slightly damaging her left eye. Each day as she went to school, she wondered, "Who's going to hit me today? Will someone throw hot soup on me today? Will it be greasy and ruin the dress my grandmother made for me? How's this day going to go?"

From October to May, the black students were more alone than ever. Not only were the paratroopers gone, but the white students who had been friendly at first had stopped being friendly. The segregationists made it clear that any white students who were friendly to the black students would be in trouble. One girl told a reporter, "I was warned that I would get it if I said anything good about the Negroes. A girl in my class—she threatened me." Some white students who tried to have lunch with their black classmates were told, "Stop that, if you don't want to get beaten up."

The nine students weren't the only targets. The segregationists were trying to disrupt the whole school. They wanted to bring school classes to a screeching halt. Then the officials would be forced to remove the nine students so that the other 1,500 could get an education.

So white teens and adults made daily phone calls to the principal's office. The messages were usually the same: a bomb is going to go off somewhere in the school. That meant the school had to stop classes and have a fire drill. (After a while, however, the officials began to ignore the calls. But they could never be sure that every call was a false alarm.) Some white parents began taking their teens out of Central. They were afraid a bomb would really go off.

Some of the white teens and adults would call the parents of the nine students, pretending to be from the school office. They'd tell the parents that their children had been injured. The parents would then panic and call or go to the school only to find out that it wasn't true.

These hoaxes, bomb threats, and attacks on the nine students made it seem as if the school officials were not controlling the school. Segregationists hoped that both black and white parents would believe the school was dangerous and remove their teenagers. Their plan almost succeeded.

By December, the students were weary of all the attacks on them. "Every morning we got up, we polished our saddle shoes and went to war," Melba said. It was a war they could win only by *not* fighting back. How much could they take? Would one of them crack? Who would it be?

The segregationists had chosen Minnijean as their main target. She was taller than the other eight students. She was the most outgoing and friendly, and she wasn't afraid to talk back to other students. They thought she'd be easy to force into fighting back. Day after day in the lunchroom, a few of them called her names and shoved chairs in her way as she walked between tables.

One Tuesday (chili day) two boys shoved chairs in her way again. Minnijean had had enough. She walked over to the boys and

dumped her lunch tray with its bowl of hot chili right on their heads.

Time seemed to come to a sudden stop in the lunchroom. Everyone sat in dead silence. It had finally happened. One of them had fought back. The cooks and janitors—all black people—had watched for weeks as the nine teenagers were picked on. But they had just seen Minnijean score a direct, well-deserved hit—a score for every black in the school. They clapped wildly as white students looked on in disbelief.

Minnijean was no stranger to Mrs. Elizabeth Huckaby's office. Mrs. Huckaby, the girls' vice principal at Central, had heard many complaints from Minnijean and the other five girls about being tripped, kicked, and called names. As she sat in Mrs. Huckaby's office, Minnijean didn't know what to expect. She was mad at herself for losing her temper and dumping her chili on the boys. She knew how important it was to try to stay cool at Central. Then Mr. Matthews came to Mrs. Huckaby's office and told Minnijean she was suspended. "What about the boys?" she snapped.

"They've been sent home to clean up," Mrs. Huckaby said, avoiding Minnijean's tearful eyes.

"Are they suspended, too?" Minnijean demanded.

"No, they're not," said Mr. Matthews, looking away from her. He and Mrs. Huckaby both knew this was unfair, but they had no proof that the boys had forced Minnijean to retaliate. Even if they had proof, they'd still have to punish Minnijean. The segregationist students had already spread the word—inside and outside Central—about what had happened. And of course, their story was that Minnijean had dumped chili on two innocent boys. Some white parents would now demand that the school do something about this "troublemaker."

"Things happen to me all the time and nobody gets suspended for it, but when I do something, I get suspended," Minnijean said bitterly. But it was useless. She could come back to Central after three days, but only if she brought her mother in to talk to Mr. Blossom, the superintendent. Since it was just one day before Christmas vacation, she'd be out until the first week in January.

■ ■ ■ ■ ■ ■

When Minnijean returned in January, she was put on probation. That meant she could stay in school as long as she did not talk back to any students who called her names or get into any fights. So, of course, the segregationists continued to pick on her. During the month, one boy dumped hot soup on her, someone spit on her, and she was called names.

One day, a white girl who had been bothering her for days followed her down the hall, stepping on her heels and calling her names. Then she bumped into Minnijean.

Stopping in her tracks, Minnijean turned around slowly, as slowly as her anger would allow. Her eyes shot a warning to the girl, but her mouth remained closed.

The girl put her hand on her hips and threatened Minnijean. "If you do that again, I'll beat you up," she said. She was acting as if the whole thing were Minnijean's fault. Minnijean turned around and kept walking. She still had enough self-control to ignore the girl. But as she headed for homeroom, the girl kept calling her names.

Then something snapped inside Minnijean. She whirled around and glared at the girl. "Don't say anything more to me, white trash," she snapped. Then she whirled back around and kept walking to her class. Out of the corner of one eye she saw one of the guardsmen. He'd been watching the whole thing but so far had done nothing to stop it.

The girl started screaming at Minnijean and threw her pocketbook, hitting the black teen in the back of the head. For the last time, Minnijean spun around, scowling. In a rage, she bent down and scooped up the girl's purse in her right hand. Like a baseball pitcher, she wound up to hit the girl with the purse, but something stopped her. A thought that it was already too late, that she had already lost the game. Her arm went limp and she dropped the purse like a used tissue on the floor.

The purse-throwing had forced the guard to act. As the white girl stooped to pick up her purse, he walked over to the two teenagers. "All right, girls," he muttered. "Let's go to the office." So off they went to Mrs. Huckaby's. "Minnijean called me 'white trash,'" the girl complained to Mrs. Huckaby.

"She's been calling me 'nigger' for a week and threw her pocketbook at me after I called her 'white trash,'" Minnijean said.

Mrs. Huckaby took the girls to Mr. Matthews's office. He reminded the teens of how serious their actions were. He asked them to make peace with each other.

"I'll apologize if she will," Minnijean said. But the other girl wouldn't apologize. Even though she knew she'd be suspended, she saw it as a victory—a victory for the segregationists. Mr. Blossom expelled Minnijean for name-calling and being in a purse-throwing fight. It was her last day at Central.

The next day, some of the white students passed out printed cards to other white students. The cards said, "One down, eight to go."

■ ■ ■ ■ ■ ■

The other eight black students made it through the rest of the year, however. After school each day, they met with Mrs. Bates at her home or talked to her on the phone. If the students were like nonviolent soldiers at war, Mrs. Bates was their commander in chief. She couldn't be in school with them because she was neither one of their parents nor a teacher. But in their daily talks, she helped them keep up their courage. She reminded them of how important it was to stay at Central High School—for their own education and for that of many other black students who would be going to white schools in the future.

Mrs. Bates listened carefully to the students

and kept records of everything that happened to them. When the students' worried parents called her, she calmed them and assured them that the teenagers would be okay. She phoned the school and scolded the officials for not protecting the students or for not treating them fairly. At one point she even called the Pentagon in Washington, D.C., to talk to the general in charge of the guards at Central. She told him she didn't like the way the guards ignored attacks on the students. After her call the general sent in more troops from the 101st Airborne Division. These troops were more fearsome to the segregationists, and there were fewer bold attacks.

With Mrs. Bates, the teenagers were able to let off steam and even laugh about some of the things that happened at Central. They said they always knew they were in for trouble, for instance, whenever Governor Faubus said anything on television or in the newspapers. He still spoke out against integration. So did members of the Mothers' League and the White Citizens' Council. When these people spoke out, the teens would groan and chuckle. Jokingly, they'd say it was time to wear their knee pads at Central, because the white teens would be fired up and there would be more attacks.

On May 27, 1958, Ernest Green—the only senior among the Little Rock Nine—graduated from Central High School. It had been a hard year for him. Like the others, he had received his share of attacks. And although he was a senior, he couldn't go to the senior prom or to any of the normal senior activities. No parties or picnics or games. He couldn't even play his saxophone in the school band. School officials felt segregationists would cause trouble if Ernest tried to take part in these activities.

As he walked across the stage at graduation, there was no cheering or applause as there had been for the 202 students before him or as there would be for the 399 students after him. There had been threats that the segregationists would not allow him to graduate. More than two hundred police officers and guards kept watch to prevent any trouble.

When his name was called, a hush spread over the audience. Many of them held their breath, fearing something horrible. Some clenched their jaws in anger. For the first time, a black student was graduating from Central. The nine teenagers had won another victory.

Was he upset that no one cheered for him? "I

didn't care," Ernest said later. "I accomplished what I'd come there for." He shook Mr. Matthews's hand, took his diploma, and walked proudly back to his seat.

Quietly, however, some people at the graduation were very proud of Ernest. Among them were his mother, his younger brother, Mrs. Bates, and Dr. Martin Luther King, Jr., who had been invited by Mrs. Bates. Among them, too, was a white student who expressed how she felt in Ernest's yearbook, *The Pic*. "I really admire you, Ernest," she wrote. "I doubt if I could have done half so well had the circumstances been reversed. May you achieve all your goals."

After graduating, Ernest was asked what it had been like to go to Central. "It's been an interesting year," he said in his usual calm, dry manner. "I've had a course in human relations firsthand." Indeed, so had all of the nine students. And so had Little Rock and the nation.

Epilogue

Seven of the students were supposed to return to Central in September of 1958—everyone except Minnijean and Ernest. But no students, black or white, returned to Central that year. Governor Faubus closed all the public schools rather than allow them to be integrated. The schools remained closed until August of 1959. By then, only Carlotta and Jefferson were left to return to Central. The others had enrolled in schools elsewhere or had graduated. Carlotta and Jefferson graduated from Central in 1960.

Over the years, more and more black students went to Central. Today, the school is fully integrated. A little more than half of the students and a third of the faculty at Central are black.

All of the Little Rock Nine went on to college and entered careers. Here is what happened to each of them.

Ernest Green became a senior vice president of a large banking company in Washington, D.C. Before that, he was Assistant Secretary of Labor, appointed by President Carter in 1977.

Melba Patillo Beals became a journalist. She had her own radio talk show in San Francisco.

Jefferson Thomas became an accounting clerk for the United States Government in Los Angeles.

Thelma Mothershed Wair became a school counselor in East St. Louis, Illinois.

Carlotta Walls Lanier became a real-estate broker in Denver, Colorado.

Terrance Roberts became a college professor in Pasadena, California.

Gloria Ray Karlmark lives in Europe, in the Netherlands. She became the editor of a computer magazine.

Minnijean Brown Trickey lives in Canada. She became a writer and is active in environmental causes.

Elizabeth Eckford returned to Little Rock to live after serving in the Army. She became a social worker.

Daisy Bates continued to fight for the rights of black people in Arkansas. She and her husband published *The Arkansas State Press* until 1959, when segregationists forced the paper to close down. Mr. Bates died in 1980. In 1983, Mrs. Bates was able to start the newspaper again.

Over the years, Mrs. Bates has been honored by many organizations throughout the country. In 1987, an integrated elementary school for 650 children in Little Rock was named for her.

Virgil Blossom was superintendent of the Little Rock schools until 1959, when he became the head of the Northeast Public Schools in San Antonio, Texas, until 1965.

Edwin A. Walker announced in 1962 that he had been "on the wrong side" in Little Rock. After resigning from the Army, Walker was an outspoken segregationist during civil rights events of the 1960s.

Orval Faubus was reelected governor of Arkansas five times. His last year in office was 1966. He ran again for governor in 1970, 1974, and 1986 but was defeated each time.

Afterword

All of the events in *Days of Courage* really happened. The facts were taken from newspaper articles, books, and documentary films. These sources, however, sometimes did not describe or show how people reacted to events—how they felt or how their voices sounded, for example. In order to bring this story to life, some of the descriptions of feelings, sounds, and appearances you have read have been made up. These descriptions, however, were inferred from the facts. None of the dialogue was made up. All of the words in quotation marks are the words that were actually spoken by the people presented in the story.

The events that occurred in Little Rock, Arkansas, in the fall of 1957 were among the first to be seen on television by millions of people. Television was still a new means of communication then. People were not used to seeing events in the real world shown on a screen in their homes. Television helped give Little Rock an important place in the memory of many people and in the history of the United States.

Notes

Page 2 Central High was the largest high school in the United States from the time it was built in 1927 until the 1940's. It could accommodate as many as 3,000 students.

Page 4 Orval E. Faubus was first elected governor in 1954. Two years later, he ran again for governor, expressing moderate views about segregation. He won that election with the support of many black voters. During his second term, he also appointed black members to the state boards and the Democratic Party committees. But as southern politicians took stronger action against integration, so did Faubus.

Page 5 Little Rock was actually among the first United States cities to comply with the Federal order to desegregate the schools. The Little Rock plan for desegregating the schools called for a "slow, gradual, and voluntary" addition of black students to white schools. This plan was opposed by the Federal District Court and also by the local chapter of the National Association for the Advancement of Colored People (NAACP) because it was neither specific nor fast enough. The White Citizen's Council was totally opposed to the plan for different reasons—it didn't want blacks and whites to attend the same schools ever.

Page 6 Teachers at Central had to cook their own food and clean up their own classrooms that day because the black workers were not allowed into the school.

Page 11 Mrs. Bates was the president of the Arkansas National Association for the Advancement of Colored People (NAACP). As a child in Huttig, Arkansas, she had gone to a poor all-black school. Her schoolbooks had been old hand-me-downs from white schools. "I knew how important an equal education was for all Negroes," she said, "to get jobs and take part in politics."

Page 12 In the 1940's and early 1950's, there were no black policemen on the Little Rock police force. Due in part to pressure created by the Bateses' newspaper, the city began to hire black policemen for the black sections of the city. Today, the Little Rock police force is integrated and has been for some years.

Page 15 Estimates of the number of people in the mob vary. Al Nall of the *Amsterdam News* reported that there were 4,500 people. Recalling the event years later, Ernest Green estimated the crowd to be from 100 to 200. *The New York Times* for September 5, 1957, said that there were 400 people in the mob. This last figure was the most commonly reported and is therefore the figure I chose to use in *Days of Courage.*

Page 15 Many of the people in the crowd were not even from Arkansas. Craig Rains, a white student, reported to Mrs. Huckaby, the Girls' Vice Principal at Central, that he noticed out-of-state license plates on some of the cars driven by people in the mob. He did not see many people he recognized as being from Little Rock.

Page 24 The reporter was Dr. Benjamin Fine, who was later attacked by the crowd because he was Jewish and from New York City. Visiting Mrs. Bates's home a few days later, he told her, "Daisy, they spat in my face. They called me a dirty Jew. I've been a marked man since the day Elizabeth tried to enter Central."

Page 25 Later, when asked what she had been called by members of the mob, Elizabeth Eckford said, "I wouldn't want to repeat those words. Some of them I never heard before, but I don't like them. I just want to try to forget it."

Page 26 The mob at Central High School was not the only one that tried to prevent black students from going to school with whites. In the middle 1950's, angry whites in Kentucky, North Carolina, Tennessee, and other states conducted protests, often violently, against the integration of schools. However, schools in three other Arkansas cities were integrated without violence.

Page 42 The mob's action actually strengthened the students' determination. Terrance Roberts said, "After seeing what these people were trying to do, I was more determined than ever to attend Central High School. I wasn't going to let anyone . . . prevent me from exercising this right, which I felt was mine."

Page 47 The mayor of Little Rock, Woodrow Wilson Mann, was alarmed by the size of the mob outside Central High on Tuesday, September 24. He sent a telegram to President Eisenhower saying, "The immediate need for Federal troops is urgent. . . . Situation is out of control and police cannot disperse the mob. . . ."

Page 47 Altogether, 11,000 soldiers were called into service by President Eisenhower. This included 1,000 paratroopers of the 101st Division and 10,000 Air and Army National Guardsmen from cities in Arkansas. Of the 10,000 National Guardsmen, 1,250 were sent to Central High. These were members of the 153rd Infantry, who were not from Little Rock. They were not the same soldiers as those called into action by Governor Faubus on September 3. Although there were black soldiers in the

101st Airborne, they were not placed on duty at Central. Instead, they were placed on reserve duty at a nearby armory.

Page 48 Watching the paratroopers come into Little Rock, Jefferson Thomas said, "When I saw the troops coming across the bridge into Little Rock, I had a feeling as if I'd been watching a movie on television, and you know the Army always wins, so everything's going to be settled. And it's a feeling like Christmas, Fourth of July, New Year's, and your birthday all rolled into one—as if you've finally found something you've been searching for for so long, you don't have to worry about it any more."

Page 49 The President was also concerned about the image of the United States in foreign countries—particularly the Soviet Union. In his speech, he mentioned that the Soviets were "gloating over this incident and using it everywhere to misrepresent our whole nation." The Soviets had apparently even broadcast a story claiming that Elizabeth Eckford had been murdered by whites.

Page 50 The students received letters and phone calls threatening that they would be lynched. But they also received thousands of letters of encouragement and support from people around the country and from foreign countries.

Page 61 Minnijean was chosen to sing a solo for the Christmas program. She rehearsed for two months and even had her mother make a dress for the performance. But she was not allowed to sing. She was told that there might be protests by the parents in the audience.

Pages 66–67 The teenagers reported the attacks, but little could be done about them. Unless a school official actually caught a white student in the act of doing something to one of the black students, the whites were rarely punished. In time, the nine teenagers learned to brush off most of the attacks, even though they continued to report them. For example, Mrs. Huckaby wrote on Friday, January 3, "After school, Elizabeth Eckford dropped by. She apologized for coming so often [to complain about attacks], but I assured her that I didn't feel she was coming too frequently. She said that except for some broken glass thrown at her during lunch, she really had had a wonderful day."

Page 75 Some whites accused Minnijean of deliberately causing trouble at Central. But most accounts support the idea that she was forced to rebel by a group of segregationist students within Central. These students were probably supported by adults outside the school. The cards passed out by some of these students that read "One down, eight to go" were printed in a way that could only have been done by an adult with typesetting equipment.

Richard Kelso lives and works in New York City where he is a staff writer for Curriculum Concepts. Mr. Kelso is also the author of *Walking for Freedom* and *Building a Dream.*